PE⬤PLE
in Time and Place

LIVING IN FAMILIES

SERIES CONSULTANTS

Dr. James F. Baumann
Professor and Head of the Department of Reading Education
College of Education
The University of Georgia
Athens, GA

Dr. Theodore Kaltsounis
Professor of Social Studies Education
University of Washington
Seattle, WA

LITERATURE CONSULTANTS

Dr. Ben A. Smith
Assistant Professor of Social Studies Education
Kansas State University
Manhattan, KS

Dr. John C. Davis
Professor of Elementary Education
University of Southern Mississippi
Hattiesburg, MS

Dr. Jesse Palmer
Assistant Professor, Department of Curriculum and Instruction
University of Southern Mississippi
Hattiesburg, MS

SILVER BURDETT GINN

MORRISTOWN, NJ • NEEDHAM, MA
Atlanta, GA • Dallas, TX • Deerfield, IL • Menlo Park, CA

SERIES AUTHORS

Dr. W. Frank Ainsley, Professor of Geography, University of North Carolina, Wilmington, N.C.

Dr. Herbert J. Bass, Professor of History, Temple University, Philadelphia, PA.

Dr. Kenneth S. Cooper, Professor of History, Emeritus, George Peabody College for Teachers, Vanderbilt University, Nashville, TN

Dr. Gary S. Elbow, Professor of Geography, Texas Tech University, Lubbock, TX

Roy Erickson, Program Specialist, K–12 Social Studies and Multicultural Education San Juan Unified School District, Carmichael, CA

Dr. Daniel B. Fleming, Professor of Social Studies Education, Virginia Polytechnic Institute and State University, Blacksburg, VA

Dr. Gerald Michael Greenfield, Professor and Director, Center for International Studies, University of Wisconsin — Parkside, Kenosha, WI

Dr. Linda Greenow, Assistant Professor of Geography, SUNY — The College at New Paltz, New York, NY

Dr. William W. Joyce, Professor of Education, Michigan State University, East Lansing, MI

Dr. Gail S. Ludwig, Geographer-in-Residence, National Geographic Society, Geography Education Program, Washington, D.C.

Dr. Michael B. Petrovich, Professor Emeritus of History, University of Wisconsin, Madison, WI

Dr. Arthur D. Roberts, Professor of Education, University of Connecticut, Storrs, CT

Dr. Christine L. Roberts, Professor of Education, University of Connecticut, Storrs, CT

Parke Rouse, Jr., Virginia Historian and Retired Executive Director of the Jamestown-Yorktown Foundation, Williamsburg, VA

Dr. Paul C. Slayton, Jr., Distinguished Professor of Education, Mary Washington College, Fredericksburg, VA

Dr. Edgar A. Toppin, Professor of History and Dean of the Graduate School, Virginia State University, Petersburg, VA

GRADE-LEVEL WRITERS/CONSULTANTS

Susan H. Grassmyer, Teacher, Shongum School, Randolph, NJ

Janet M. Hogan, Teacher, East School, New Canaan, CT

Hazel Tseng Hsieh, Teacher, Mohansic School, Yorktown Heights, NY

Charleen M. Kaaen, Teacher, Edison Elementary School, Walla Walla, WA

Margaret Ricciardi, Teacher, Woodland School, Convent Station, NJ

ACKNOWLEDGMENTS

Excerpt from *Columbus* by Ingri & Edgar Parin D'Aulaire, copyright © 1955 by Doubleday, a division of Bantam, Doubleday, Dell Publishing Group, Inc. Used by permission of the publisher.

Excerpt and illustrations from *Make Way for Ducklings* by Robert McCloskey. Copyright 1941, renewed © 1969 by Robert McCloskey. All rights reserved. Reprinted by permission of Viking Penguin, a division of Penguin Books USA, Inc.

"Wake Up!" by Eva Grant, from *Poetry Place Anthology.* Copyright © 1983 by Scholastic, Inc. Reprinted by permission of Scholastic, Inc.

From *Stone Soup* by Marcia Brown. Reprinted with permission of Charles Scribner's Sons, an imprint of Macmillan Publishing Company. Copyright 1947 Marcia Brown; copyright renewed © 1975 Marcia Brown.

CONTENTS

The Granger Collection

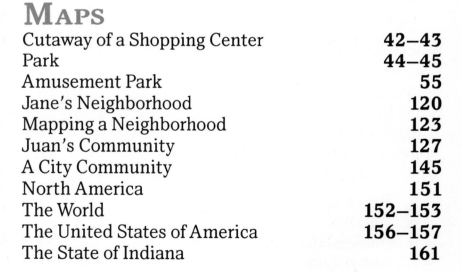

CHARTS AND TIME LINES

GRAPHS AND TABLES

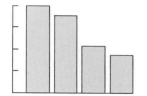

SPECIAL FEATURES
LITERATURE

PEN PALS

CITIZENSHIP AND AMERICAN VALUES

SKILLBUILDERS

SCHOOL

New Words

school

alike

alone

different

globe

rule

group

2

How Do We Get to School?

Pam is excited.
It is her first day of **school**.
Pam is in first grade.

Pam rides on the school bus.
Mr. Lee is the bus driver.
He makes sure everyone is safe.
The children sit in their seats.

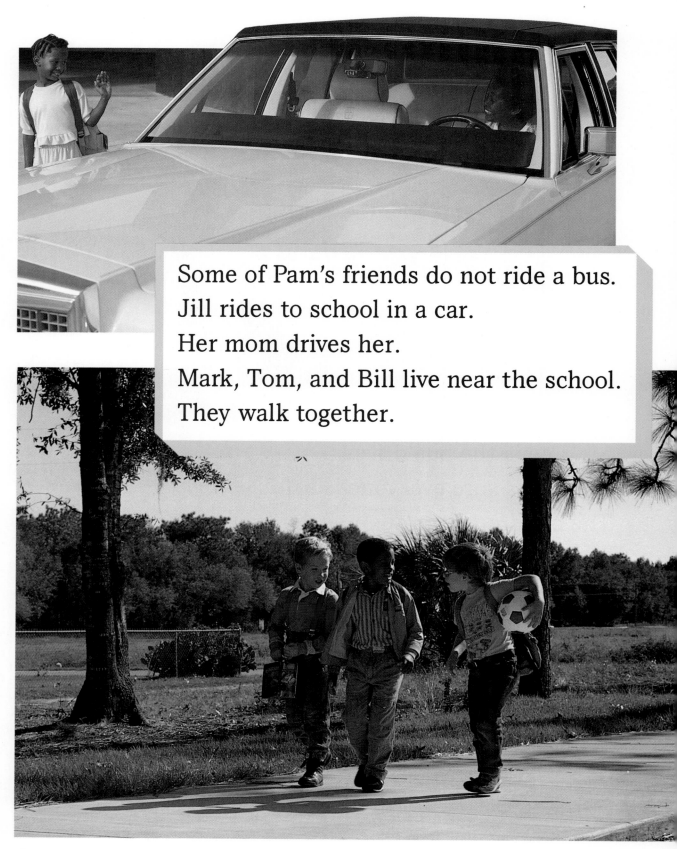

Some of Pam's friends do not ride a bus.
Jill rides to school in a car.
Her mom drives her.
Mark, Tom, and Bill live near the school.
They walk together.

The crossing guard tells them when to cross the street.
She helps children get to school too.

Review

Read and Think

1. Name some ways to get to school.
2. Who helps you get to school?

Skills Check

Look at the picture on page 7.
How does the crossing guard help the children?

Who Are the People at School?

This is a first-grade class.
Pam is part of the class.
The class learns together.
Mrs. Johnson is the teacher.
She helps the class learn.

The class walked around the school.

The class met Mr. Diaz.

He is the principal.

The principal is the head of the school.

Mr. Jones is the librarian.
He works in the school library.
He helps the class choose books.
Sometimes Mr. Jones reads to the class.

Mrs. Young is the nurse.
She helps sick people.
She also helps people
who get hurt.

These people work in the school too.
Can you tell what they do?

Review

Read and Think

1. What does a teacher do in school?
2. Who are the workers in your school?

Skills Check

Look at the top picture on page 10.
What does Mr. Jones use to do his job?

Why Do Schools Have Rules?

Ding! Ding! Ding!
It was a fire drill.
Rules told the class what to do.
The class quickly got in a line.
No one talked.
The class went outside.

Schools have many rules.
Rules help keep everyone safe.
Some rules tell children what to do.

Some rules are for a class.
Rules help the children work in the room.

Rules help children play together. Children use rules to play fairly.

Lesson 3 — Review

Read and Think

1. What do rules tell you?
2. What are the rules in your school?

Skills Check

Look at the picture on page 14.
How are rules helping the children?

How Can Rules Help Us?

We have learned about rules.
Rules help the class work together.
Peter and Jim are angry.
They both want all the new markers.

The class made some rules about the markers. The rules tell how to use the markers in the classroom.

Marker Rules
1.

Thinking for Yourself

1. What marker rules do you think the class made?
2. What other rules might help the class?
3. What rules help your class?

How Are Children Alike and Different?

All About Us

Mrs. Johnson's class made a book.
It tells about the children.
This picture shows some of the children.
They are **alike** in some ways.
All the children are in first grade.

The children are **different** in some ways.
<u>Different</u> means not the same.
Some of the children have dark hair.
Some of the children have light hair.
In what other ways are they different?

by Mrs. Johnson's Class

Sometimes we like to do the same things.

Here is another page from the book.
The children are alike and
different in what they like to do.
They all like music class.

Some children like other things too.

Sometimes we like to do different things.

Each of us is special.

Review

Read and Think

1. What does <u>different</u> mean?

2. How are you and other children alike?

Skills Check

Look at the pictures on page 21.

How are the children different?

What Do We Learn in School?

Pam and her class are busy.
They learn many things in school.

They read and write stories.
They learn about numbers.

The class learns about the **globe** too.
The globe is a model of the earth.
The globe shows water and land.
Water is blue on this globe.

The class learns about new places at school.
The children find the places on the globe.

Sometimes Pam works **alone**.
Sometimes she is part of a **group**.

Pam has friends at school.
She works and plays with them.
Pam has fun in school.

Review

Read and Think

1. What does Pam do in school?
2. How is Pam's school like your school?

Skills Check

Think about what you learn in school.
List the things you do in one day.

A. Using the New Words

Find the picture that best matches each word.

1. school _____ **A.**

2. alike _____ **B.**

3. group _____

4. different _____

5. globe _____

6. alone _____ **C.**  **D.**

7. rule _____

E.  **F.**  **G.**

B. Remembering What You Read

Answer these questions about the unit.

1. What does Pam's class do in school?
2. What do rules tell people?
3. Look at the pictures below.

   What other things can you do alone?

   What other things can you do in a group?

C. Summarizing the Unit

Make a puppet of a worker in your school.

Tell the class about your worker.

Why did you choose this worker?

How are the workers in your school alike?

SKILLBUILDER

Understanding Traffic Lights

 A ## Why Do I Need This Skill?

Streets can be busy places.
Traffic lights help you use streets safely.

 B ## Learning the Skill

There are three colors in a traffic light.
There is a rule for each color.

A red light means stop.

A yellow light means be careful.

A green light means go.

Practicing the Skill

Look at the three traffic lights in the box.
There is a letter under each light.
Find the letter that matches each rule.

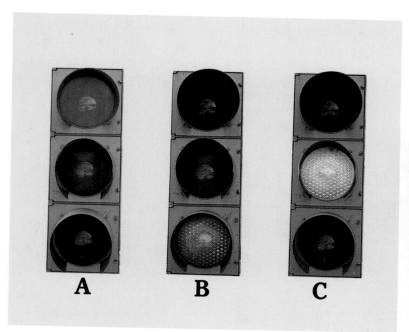

A B C

1. Go. _____
2. Stop. _____
3. Be careful. _____

D **Applying the Skill**

Look at the traffic light in the picture.
Can the person cross the street now?

Unit 2 FAMILY

New Words

family

change

map

house
street
grass

map key

farm

What Is a Family?

A **family** is a special group of people.
Everyone is a member of a family.

Families are different in some ways.
Families are different sizes.
Sometimes the whole family does
not live together.

Family members help each other.
Tom is helping Tim with the train.
Nina is learning to ride a bike.

Family members show they love
each other in many ways.
A hug is one way to show love.

Review

Read and Think

1. How are families different?

2. How do you help your family?

Skills Check

Write a story about a special day you had
with your family.

How Do Families Change?

Dan's family had a **change**.
A change is when something
does not stay the same.
Dan has a new baby sister.
His family is bigger now.

Dan told the class about his new sister.
Then the class talked about other changes.
Some changes make people happy.
Some changes make people sad.

Meg's family moved
to a new house.
It was a change for
her family.
Meg likes her new
house.

There was a change in Len's family.
His brother went away to school.
Len misses his brother.

Jill's grandfather came to live with her family. She likes seeing him all the time.

Lesson 2 —————— Review ——————

Read and Think

1. What is a change?

2. Name one change your family has had.

Skills Check

Look at the top picture on page 40.
How can you tell this family moved?

What Is a Map?

Dave and his family went
to a shopping center.
They went to the bank first.
Then they went to the pet shop.
The pet shop is near the bank.

Next they went to the sports shop.
The sports shop is far from the bank.
Dave looked into the shoe store.
The sports shop is to the right of the shoe store.
The restaurant is to the left of the shoe store.

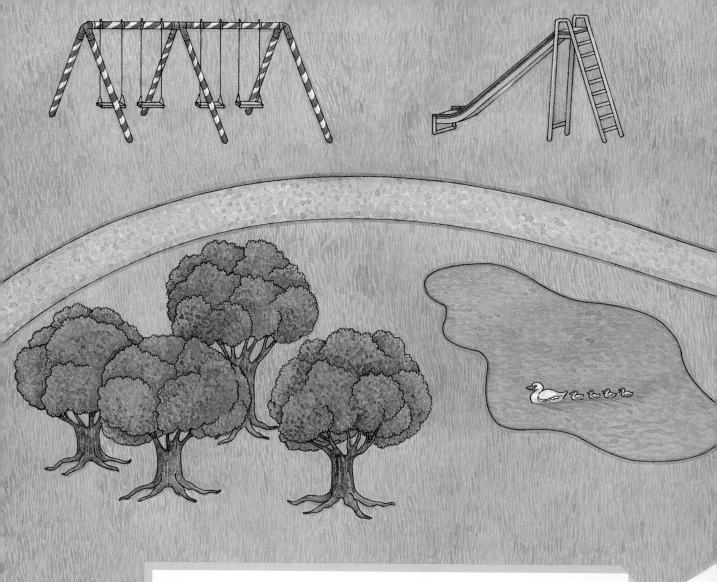

Dave and his family went to a park too.
This is a **map** of the park.
A map is a special kind of drawing.
Maps tell you where different places are.
A **map key** helps you understand the map.
Find the picture for table in the map key.
Now find the tables on the map.
How many tables are there in the park?

44

Map key

	Swings
	Slide
	Sandbox
	Path
	Table
	Pond
	Tree
	Carousel

Lesson 3 ——— Review ———

Read and Think

1. What does a map tell you?
2. Tell where you would play in the park and why.

Skills Check

Look at the map on pages 44 and 45.

What is near the slide?

What Do Family Members Do Together?

Families work and play together.
There are different ways to work and play.
Family members choose what they will do together.

Mark and his family help each other.
They work in the yard.
The family plays games too.
The family does many things together.

PEN PALS

Mark and George are pen pals.
They write to each other
about their families.

Dear Mark,

It is fun to live in London.
My family and I have been busy.
We ride double decker buses.
We play football in the park.
We shop at the markets on the street.
I like to buy fresh bread for teatime.
Write back soon.

Your friend,
George

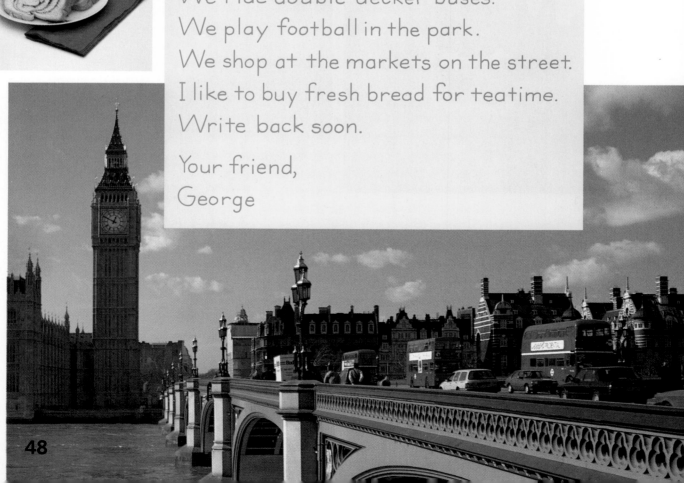

Sometimes families take trips.
Jan's family visits new places together.
Jan likes these special trips.

Lesson 4

Review

Read and Think

1. What does each family choose?
2. What do you do with your family?

Skills Check

Look at the pictures on pages 46 and 47.
How are the families alike?

What Were Families like Long Ago?

My name is Anna.
My family and I live on a **farm**.
We care for animals and grow corn to sell.

My father and my brother work in the field.
My mother makes our clothes and cooks.
I help my mother.

There are many jobs to do on our farm.
We work together to do some of the jobs.

Friends come to our house too.
We all like to dance.
We have fun when our friends visit.

Review

Read and Think

1. What kinds of jobs are there on a farm?
2. What jobs do you do that are like Anna's?

Skills Check

Look at the picture on pages 50 and 51.
How is Anna's house like your home?

A. Using the New Words

Find the picture that best matches each word.

1. farm _____

2. map _____

3. change _____

4. family _____

5. map key _____

A.

B.

C.

D. MAP KEY

house

street

grass

E.

B. Remembering What You Read

Answer these questions about the unit.
1. What is a family member?
2. What kinds of changes can families have?
3. How is your family different from Anna's family?

C. Summarizing the Unit

Look at the park map above.
1. What can families do in the park?
2. What would you do with your family?

 # Why Do I Need This Skill?

Everything happens in order.

Order helps us know how things happen.

Order helps us learn about new things.

 # Learning the Skill

Some words tell us about order.

<u>First</u>, <u>next</u>, <u>then</u>, and <u>last</u> tell about order.

This story is in order.

<u>First</u> Mark ate dinner.

<u>Next</u> he wrote to his pen pal.

<u>Then</u> he read a story.

<u>Last</u> he went to bed.

Practicing the Skill

Jan and her family went on a trip.
Find the sentence for each picture.
1. Next they packed the car.
2. First they made their lunch.
3. Last they ate the lunch.
4. Then they went to the lake.

 Applying the Skill

Draw four pictures in order.
Write the correct order word under each picture.

New Words

food

needs

shelter

clothing

apartment

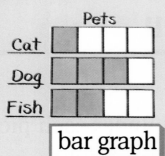
wants

	Pets		
Cat			
Dog			
Fish			

bar graph

What Are Needs and Wants?

All people have **needs**.

A need is something people must have to live.

Food is a need.

People eat food to be healthy.

Clothing is a need.
Clothing protects people
from the weather.
All people need a **shelter**.
A shelter is a place to live.

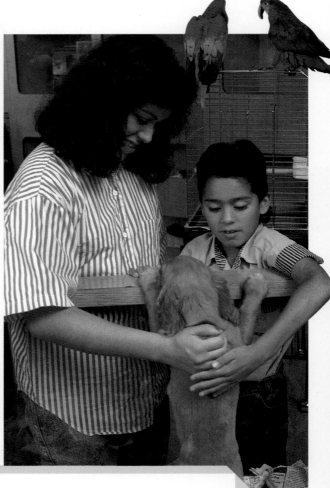

People have **wants** too.

A want is something a person would like to have.

Wants are not the same for all people.

Mary's family would like a new car.
What is a want that you have?

Lesson 1
Review

Read and Think

1. How are wants and needs different?
2. What wants does your class have?

Skills Check

Find the new words on pages 60 and 61.
Put the words in ABC order.

How Can We Help Other People?

Trevor Ferrell heard about a problem.

The problem was that some people needed homes.

Trevor wanted to help the people.

One cold night he met a man without a home.

He gave the man a pillow and a blanket.

Trevor wanted the man to stay warm.

64

More people needed Trevor's help.
Trevor wanted to help them too.
He asked other people to work with him.
They gave Trevor food and blankets.
Trevor gave them to people without homes.

Thinking for Yourself

1. Why did some people need Trevor's help?

2. Why, do you think, did other people help Trevor?

3. How can you help other people?

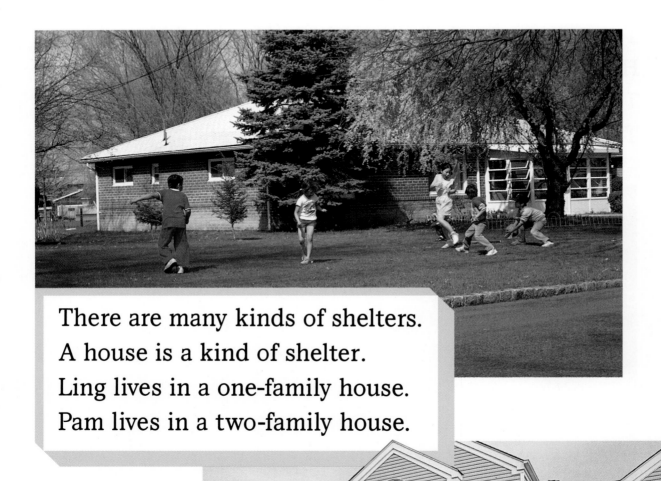

What Kinds of Shelters Are There?

There are many kinds of shelters.
A house is a kind of shelter.
Ling lives in a one-family house.
Pam lives in a two-family house.

Sue and Tom live in a tall building.
The building has many **apartments**.
Each apartment is a shelter.
Sue and Tom live in different apartments.

There are other kinds of shelters.
Some of the shelters are in warm places.

Some of the shelters are in cold places.
How are the shelters different?

Lesson 2

Review

Read and Think

1. Name three kinds of shelters.
2. Which shelter is like your shelter?

Skills Check

Look at the pictures on page 68.
How can you tell the shelters are in warm places?

FROM
MAKE WAY FOR DUCKLINGS
BY ROBERT McCLOSKEY

People and animals need homes.
The ducks in this story need a home.
Where do you think they will look?

So they flew over Beacon Hill and round the
State House, but there was no place there.

They looked in Louisburg Square, but there was no water to swim in.

Then they flew over
the Charles River.
"This is better,"
quacked Mr. Mallard.

"That island looks like
a nice quiet place,
and it's only a little way
from the Public Garden."

"Yes," said Mrs. Mallard, remembering the peanuts. "That looks like just the right place to hatch ducklings."

What Do You Think?

Why was the island the best place for a home?
How do people choose their homes?

Where Do We Get Food?

The Roberts family buys food in different places.
Sometimes the family goes to a supermarket.
A supermarket has many kinds of foods.

The family goes to special stores too.
Special stores sell one kind of food.
A bakery is a special store.
A cheese shop is a special store.

Some farmers grow food for many people.
The farms have large fields for their crops.
Farmers sell their crops to stores.

Some farmers have farm stands too.
The farmers sell food from the farm.
The Roberts family likes fresh vegetables.
The family buys vegetables at a farm stand.

This is a **bar graph**.
A bar graph tells a story.
It tells how much or how many.
This graph tells how many trips the
Roberts family made for food.
One box is colored for each trip
to a place.
How many trips were made to
the farm stand?

Trips to Buy Food in a Week

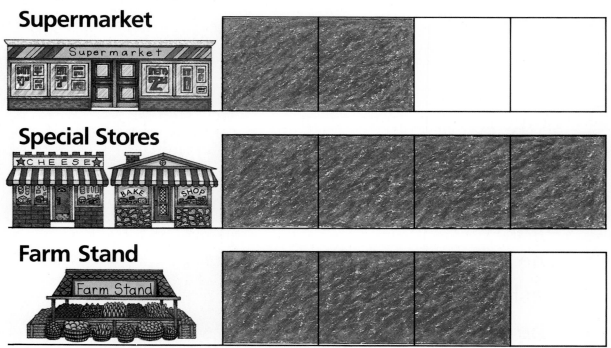

Supermarket

Special Stores

Farm Stand

Bill likes bar graphs.
He is ready to make a graph.

Lesson 3

Review

Read and Think

1. Where does the family buy food?
2. Where do you buy food?

Skills Check

Look at the graph on page 80.

How many trips were made to the supermarket?

How Do We Get Clothing?

Jon and his father are at a clothing store.
The store sells clothes in many sizes.
Jon needs bigger clothes.
They will buy the size he needs.

Mrs. Smith works with yarn.
She knits sweaters.
She sells some of her sweaters.
Other sweaters she gives to her family.
Mrs. Smith made a sweater for Kevin.

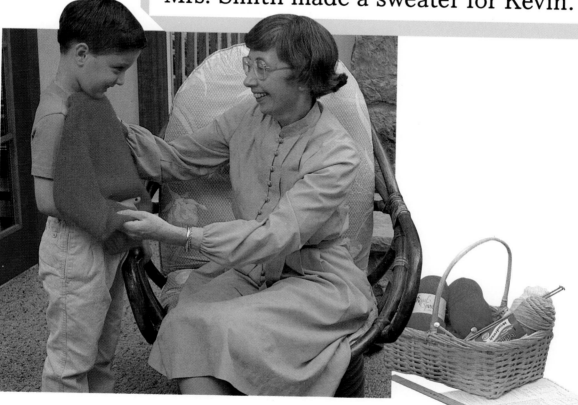

Mrs. Long sews clothes for her family.
She buys some cloth.
Then she cuts the cloth into pieces.
Mrs. Long sews the pieces together.

Jen tries on her new skirt.
The new skirt fits her well.

Review

Read and Think

1. Where does Jon get his clothes?

2. Where do you get your clothes?

Skills Check

Look at the pictures on pages 84 and 85.

List three things Mrs. Long needs to make a skirt.

A. Using the New Words

Find the picture that best matches each word.

1. needs ____

2. apartment ____

3. clothing ____

4. shelter ____

5. bar graph ____

6. wants ____

7. food ____

A.

B.

C.

D.

E.

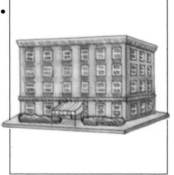

F.

G.

B. **Remembering What You Read**

Answer these questions about the unit.

1. Name three kinds of needs.
2. How are shelters alike and different?
3. Why are people's wants different?

 C. **Summarizing the Unit**

A.   **B.**   **C.**

Look at the pictures above.

Use the letters to put the pictures in order.

First _____   Next _____   Last _____

Where could the family buy the food it needs?

Grouping Words

A Why Do I Need This Skill?

Sometimes we can make word groups.
The words in the group are alike in some way.
The groups help us learn about the words.

B Learning the Skill

You learned about needs and wants.
Here are word groups for needs and wants.

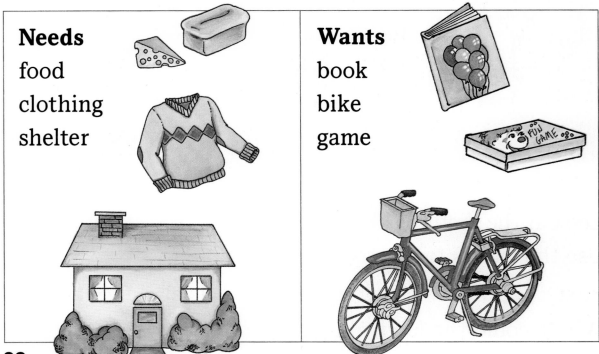

Needs
food
clothing
shelter

Wants
book
bike
game

Practicing the Skill

Look at the word groups on this page.

People

teacher

nurse

Places

school

home

1. Copy the groups onto a piece of paper.

2. Put these words in the correct group.

friend   park   store   principal

3. Think of more people and places.
Put each one in the correct group.

 Applying the Skill

Look at the words in the box below.

sweater   shirt   pants   coat

Name this word group.

89

New Words

travel

factory

service

goods

Going to School

Bus	👤👤👤👤👤
Car	👤👤👤
Walk	👤👤

pictograph

What Are Goods and Services?

Many people work each day.
The work they do is their job.
There are different kinds of jobs.
Some people make things.
The things they make are
called **goods**.

These workers are making goods.
Machines help them work faster.
Sometimes many people work
together to make goods.
Each job is important.

Some workers do things for people.
The job they do is a **service**.
A barber cuts hair.
A doctor helps you stay healthy.

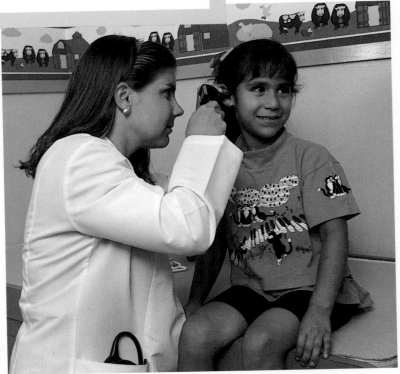

Many people send packages to each other.
This worker brings people their packages.

Review

Read and Think

1. What are goods?
2. Name some other service jobs.

Skills Check

Look at the pictures on pages 92 and 93.
How are the goods being made?

Lesson 2

Where Do People Work?

People work in different places.
A school is one place to work.
A **factory** is another place to work.
The workers in a factory make goods.

Some people work in stores.
Others work in banks.
Some people load and unload
ships at a dock.
There are many places to work.

Places Where People in Our Families Work

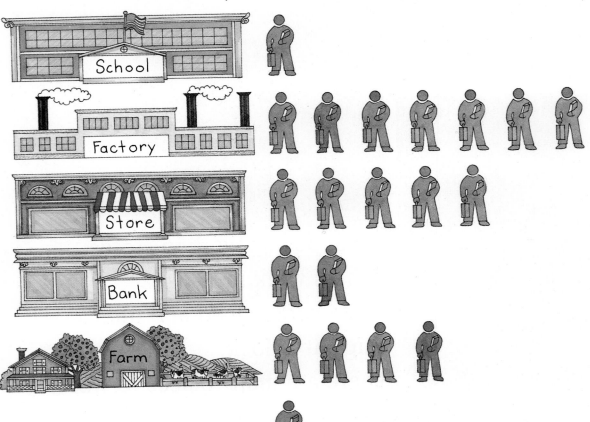

stands for one worker.

Mrs. Johnson's class talked about workers. The children made a **pictograph** about workers in their families.

A pictograph uses pictures to show how much or how many.

There is one ![worker icon] for each worker.

How many store workers are there?

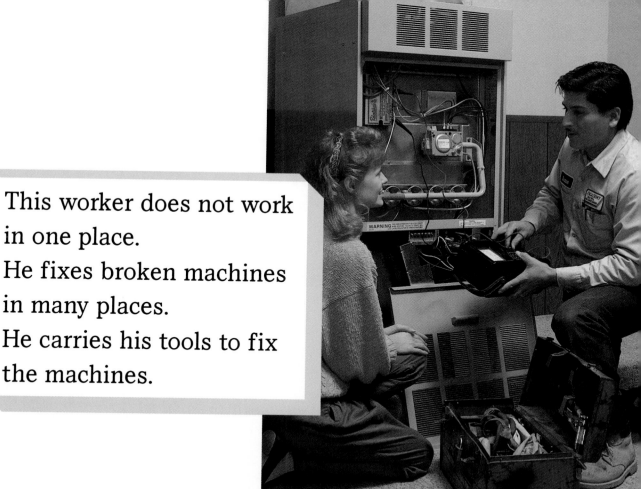

This worker does not work in one place.
He fixes broken machines in many places.
He carries his tools to fix the machines.

Lesson 2

Review

Read and Think

1. What is made in a factory?
2. Tell where you would like to work and why.

Skills Check

Look at the pictograph on page 98.
How many more people work in factories than on farms?

Lesson 3

How Are Sneakers Made?

Mrs. Johnson's class went to a factory.
The factory makes sneakers.
Many workers are needed to make sneakers.

1 Rubber is used for the bottoms of sneakers.
A worker reads a recipe for yellow rubber.
The recipe tells him how to make the rubber.

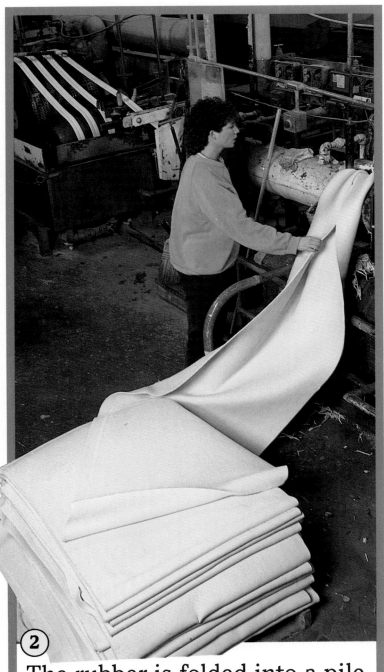

3

Each piece makes
the bottom of
a sneaker.

2

The rubber is folded into a pile.
Then the pile is cut into pieces.

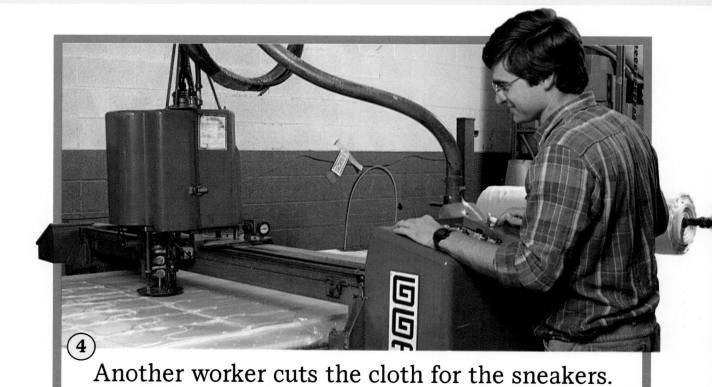

④ Another worker cuts the cloth for the sneakers.

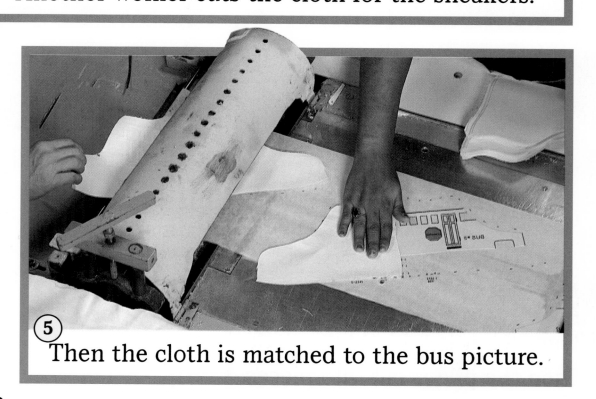

⑤ Then the cloth is matched to the bus picture.

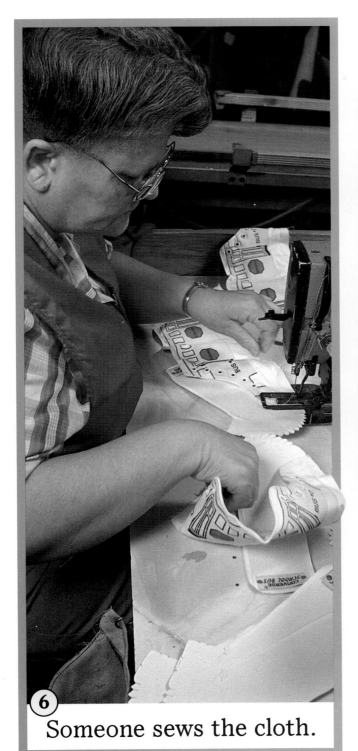

6 Someone sews the cloth.

7 There are cushions in sneakers. A worker glues the cloth to the cushions.

8 Next the shoe is dipped in a special glue.

9 Then rubber pieces are added to the sneakers.

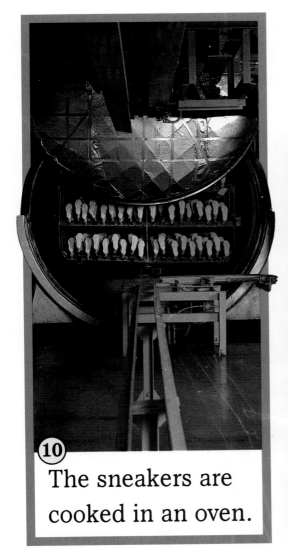

10 The sneakers are cooked in an oven.

11 Shoelaces are added to each pair of sneakers.

(12) Some workers put the sneakers in boxes.

(13) Trucks take the sneakers to many stores.

14 The class has seen the sneakers in stores.
Pam's friends each bought a pair of sneakers.

<u>Lesson 3</u>

Review

Read and Think

1. How do workers help to make the sneakers?
2. Why is it important for all the workers to do their jobs?

Skills Check

You are going to work in a sneaker factory.
Write about your new job and what you will do.

107

How Do People Travel to Work?

Travel means to go from one place to another.
Long ago travel took a long time.
People had to live near their jobs.
People used horses and trains to travel.

Today many people must travel to work.
They do not live near their jobs.
Cars and buses help people travel to work.
Mr. Hill rides a bus to his job.
Mrs. Hill drives a car to her job.

There are other ways to travel too.
Some workers take a boat to work.
Other workers take a train.

People travel on airplanes too.
An airplane is another way to go places.
Airplanes are much faster than cars.

Lesson 4 ——— Review ———

Read and Think

1. Name some ways people travel.
2. Which way do you like to travel and why?

Skills Check

Look at the pictures on page 108.
How are the train and the wagon different?

A. Using the New Words

Find the picture that best matches each word.

1. factory ____

2. travel ____

3. pictograph ____

4. goods ____

5. service ____

A.

B.

Going to School

Bus 🚶🚶🚶🚶🚶
Car 🚶🚶🚶
Walk 🚶🚶

C.

D.

E.

B. Remembering What You Read

Answer these questions about the unit.

1. Name some places where people work.
2. How do people travel today?
3. How is working in a factory different from working in a bank?

C. Summarizing the Unit

Write a story about a job you would like.

1. Where would you work?
2. Why would you like that job?

 ## A Why Do I Need This Skill?

Directions tell you what to do.
Following directions helps you do things the right way.

 ## B Learning the Skill

Directions helped the workers make sneakers.

The workers had to do their jobs in order.

Here are some of the directions.

1. Use the recipe to make the rubber.
2. Cut the cloth for the sides.
3. Glue the pieces together.
4. Cook the sneakers.

Practicing the Skill

Follow the directions below.

1. Get out a piece of paper.
2. Write your name on the top.
3. Draw a sneaker with your pencil.
4. Color the sneaker blue or red.

 Applying the Skill

Write the directions for making a sandwich.
Ask a friend to read your directions.

NEIGHBORHOODS AND COMMUNITIES

New Words

community

directions

neighbor

neighborhood

city

Kinds of Clothing

Clothing	Summer	Winter
Shorts	X	
Mittens		X

table

THE POSTMARK

What Is a Neighborhood?

A **neighborhood** is a group of homes.
The homes are near each other.
People who live near each other
are **neighbors**.

Neighbors can help each other.
Mrs. James will help her neighbor
rake leaves.
Neighbors can work together too.
These neighbors are building a play area.
The children will soon have a new
place to play.

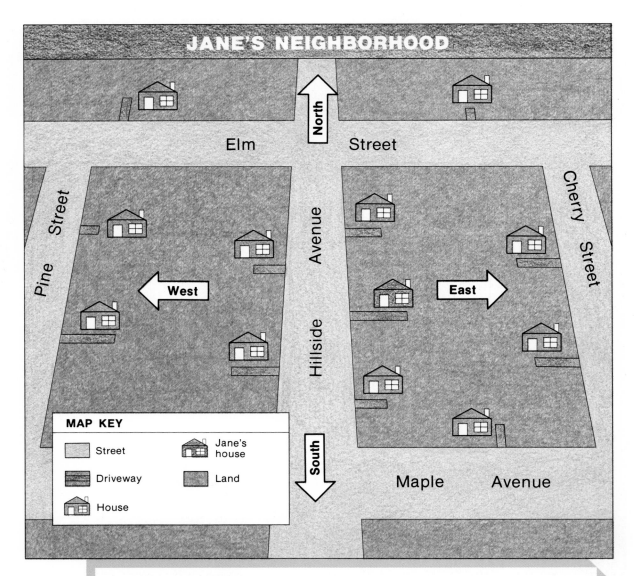

Look at the map on this page.

It shows Jane's neighborhood.

There are **directions** on this map.

Directions help people find places.

North, south, east, and west are directions.

North and south are opposite directions.

East and west are opposite directions.

Use the map on page 120.
Kim is on Maple Avenue.
In which direction will she walk
to go to Jane's house?

Review

Read and Think

1. Name the four directions.
2. What do you do with your neighbors?

Skills Check

Look at the map on page 120.
Which street is east of Jane's house?

How Is a Map Like a Picture?

A helicopter flies high in the air.
This picture was taken from a helicopter.
The picture shows Ann's neighborhood.

This is a map of Ann's neighborhood.
Use the map key to find Ann's house
on the map.

Ann's house is yellow on the map.

Can you find Ann's house in the picture?

How are the map and the picture alike?

Ann has a new pen pal named Rosa.
Rosa wrote to Ann about her neighborhood.

Dear Ann,

My family and I live in Chile.
Our neighborhood is near the water.
My father catches fish for his job.
Many of our neighbors fish too.
Our neighborhood has a party in June.
It is a party for people who fish.
We are thankful for the sea.

Your friend,
Rosa

Ann is busy working and playing
in her neighborhood.
She does many things with her neighbors.

Lesson 2
Review

Read and Think

1. How was the picture of Ann's neighborhood taken?
2. Why does a map need a map key?

Skills Check

Look at pages 122 and 123.
How is the picture different from the map?

What Is a Community?

Juan lives in a neighborhood.
His neighborhood is part
of a **community**.
A community is a group
of neighborhoods.
The map on page 127 shows
Juan's community.

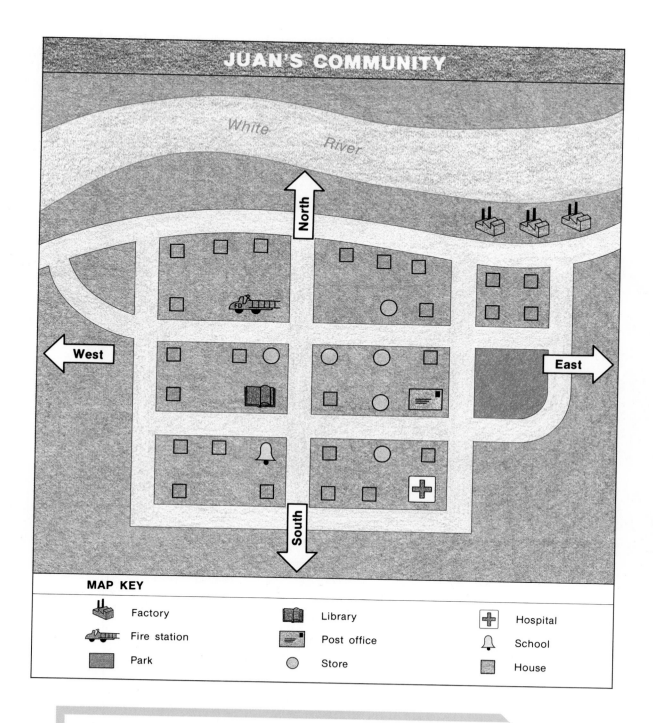

JUAN'S COMMUNITY

MAP KEY

Factory		Library		Hospital	
Fire station		Post office		School	
Park		Store		House	

The post office is one special place in the community.
What other special places do you see?

The school is a place for children to learn.
The library is a place for everyone to learn.
The stores sell people the things they need.

Some communities have places to play.
Juan likes to play in the park.

Review

Read and Think

1. Name three special places in a community.

2. Tell about your community.

Skills Check

Look at the map on page 127.

Which direction is the post office from the park?

FROM
Stone Soup
BY MARCIA BROWN

Three hungry soldiers went to a poor village.
The people would not share their food.
The soldiers decided to make stone soup.
They started with a pot and some water.

"And now, if you please, three round,

smooth stones."

Those were easy

enough to find.

The peasants'

eyes grew round

as they watched

the soldiers

drop the stones

into the pot.

"Any soup needs salt and pepper," said the
soldiers, as they began to stir.
Children ran to fetch salt
and pepper.
"Stones like these generally
make good soup.
But oh, if there were carrots
it would be much better."
"Why I think I have a carrot
or two," said Francoise,
and off she ran.
She came back with her
apron full of carrots from
the bin beneath the red quilt.

"A good stone soup should have cabbage,"
said the soldiers as they sliced the carrots
into the pot.
"But no use asking for what you don't have."

"I think I could find a cabbage somewhere,"
said Marie, and she hurried home.
Back she came
with three cabbages
from the cupboard
under the bed.

"If we only had a bit of beef and a few potatoes,
this soup would be good enough
for a rich man's table."
The peasants thought that over.

They remembered their potatoes and the
sides of beef hanging in the cellars.
They ran to fetch them.
A rich man's soup—and all from a few stones.
It seemed like magic!

What Do You Think?

What happened when the people worked together?

Who Are Community Workers?

"Mom, workers are fixing the road!"
said Joe.
"They are community workers," said Mom.
"Community workers help the community.
It will be much easier for us to drive now."

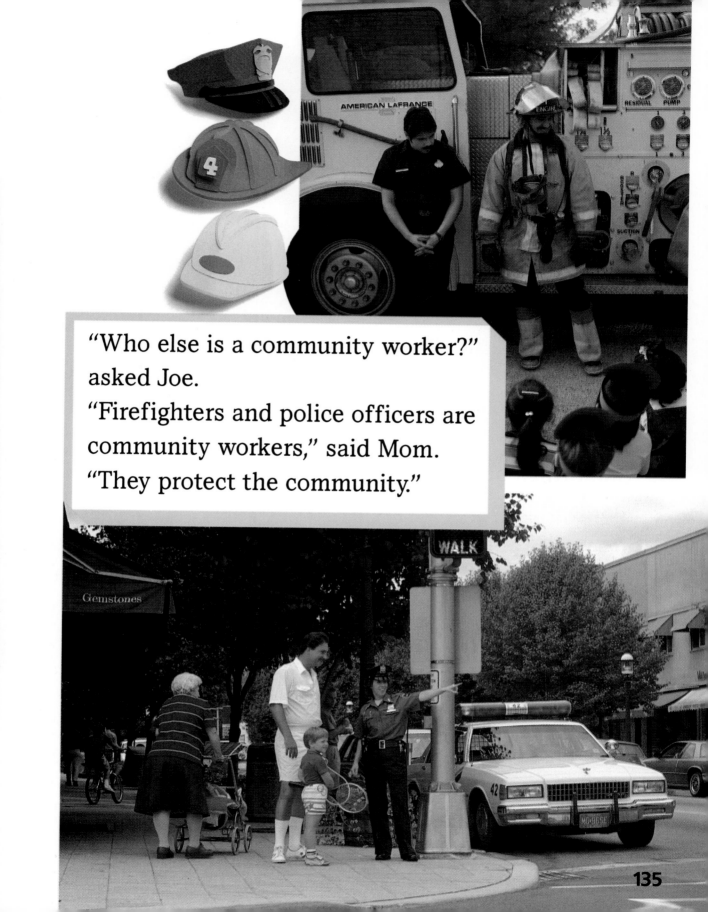

"Who else is a community worker?" asked Joe.

"Firefighters and police officers are community workers," said Mom. "They protect the community."

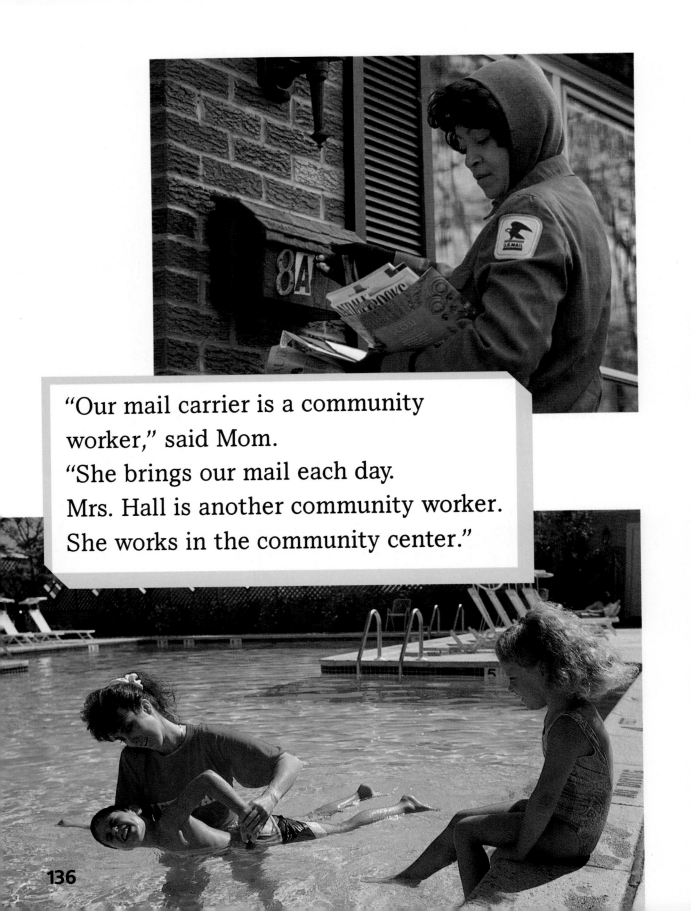

"Our mail carrier is a community
worker," said Mom.
"She brings our mail each day.
Mrs. Hall is another community worker.
She works in the community center."

"Workers cleaned the streets," said Joe.
"They must be community workers too.
The streets look much nicer now.
Many workers help our community."

Review

Read and Think

1. Name some community workers.
2. How do community workers help you?

Skills Check

Write about a time you saw a community
worker helping someone.

What Kinds of Communities Are There?

Jim lives in a farm community.
A farm needs a big piece of land.
Jim's neighbors live on nearby farms.
Most of the people in the community
work on farms.
The workers live near their jobs.

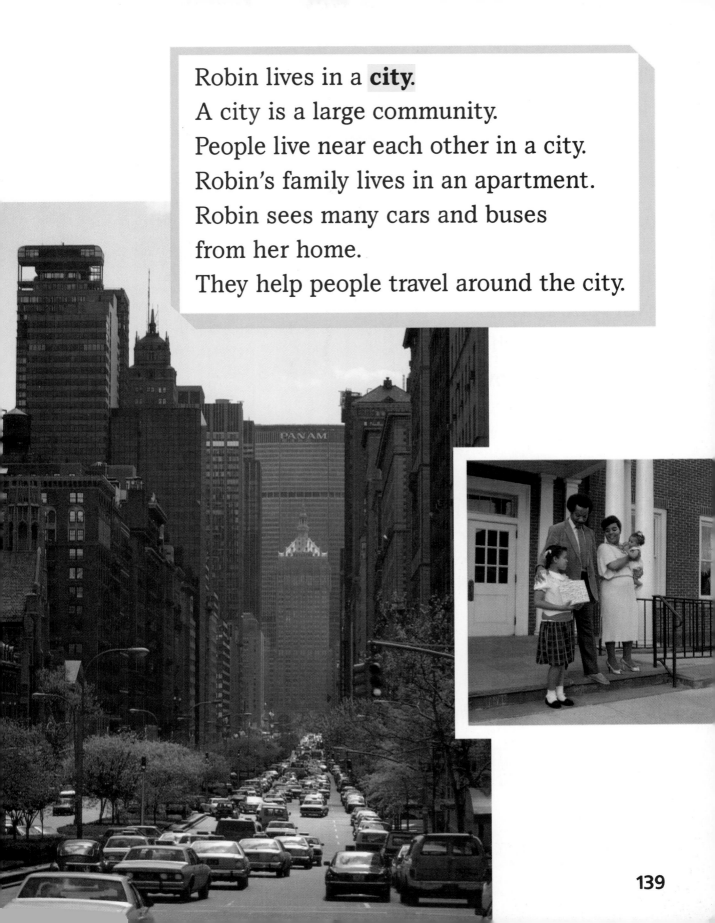

Robin lives in a **city**.
A city is a large community.
People live near each other in a city.
Robin's family lives in an apartment.
Robin sees many cars and buses
from her home.
They help people travel around the city.

This poem is about a farm and the city.
How are the two places different?

Wake Up!

In the country
Everyone knows
It's morning when
The rooster crows.

140

But the city's
A different matter!
You're sure to hear
Garbage cans clatter,
Taxis toot,
Buses roar,
A paper slap
Against your door.

In country or city,
Morning sounds say,
"Wake up! Here comes
Another day."

Eva Grant

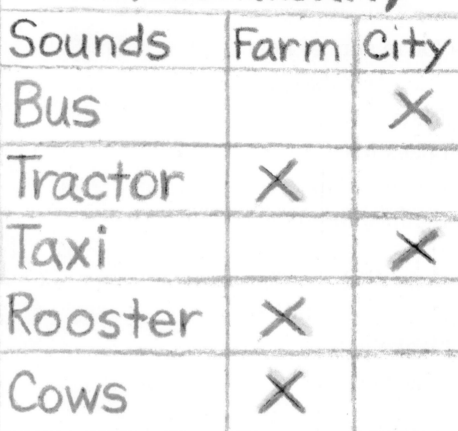

Sounds You Hear in a Community		
Sounds	Farm	City
Bus		X
Tractor	X	
Taxi		X
Rooster	X	
Cows	X	

The poem tells about different sounds.
This **table** shows some of the sounds.
A table is one way to tell about something.
You will hear taxis and buses in a city.
You will hear roosters on a farm.
What else will you hear on a farm?

Look at the pictures above.
In which kind of community will
you find each picture?

Review

Read and Think

1. How are cities and farms different?

2. Tell about your community.

Skills Check

Look at the table on page 142.
Where will you hear tractors?

A. Using the New Words

Find the picture that best matches each word.

1. city   ——
2. table   ——
3. community ——
4. neighbors ——
5. neighborhood ——
6. directions ——

A.

B.

C.

D.

E.

F.

Kinds of Animals		
Animals	Pet	Zoo
Dog	X	
Tiger		X
Zebra		X

B. Remembering What You Read

Answer these questions about the unit.

1. Name at least three community workers.
2. How are neighborhoods alike?
   How are they different?

C. Summarizing the Unit

Look at the map below.

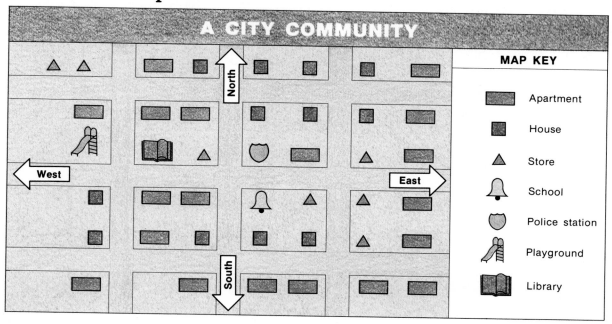

1. Is the police station north or south
   of the school?
2. How is this community different
   from your community?

145

 A # Why Do I Need This Skill?

Main ideas tell what a picture or story is about.
They help us understand what we see or read.

 B # Learning the Skill

The picture below shows community workers.
The main idea is that these workers help us.
Most stories have a main idea too.
The main idea can be one sentence.
The other sentences tell about the idea.

C Practicing the Skill

Read the story and find the main idea.

Communities have special places.
Schools are where children learn.
Stores sell things to people.
Parks are for playing or resting.
Factories and offices are for working.

D Applying the Skill

1. Draw a picture to show this main idea:
   "A neighborhood is a group of homes."
2. Write three sentences about the main idea.

Unit 6 OUR COUNTRY

New Words

ocean

continent

West Virginia

state

Congress

law

symbol

natural resources

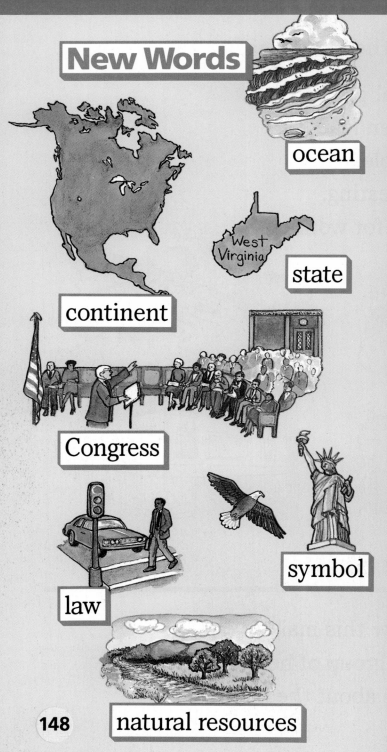

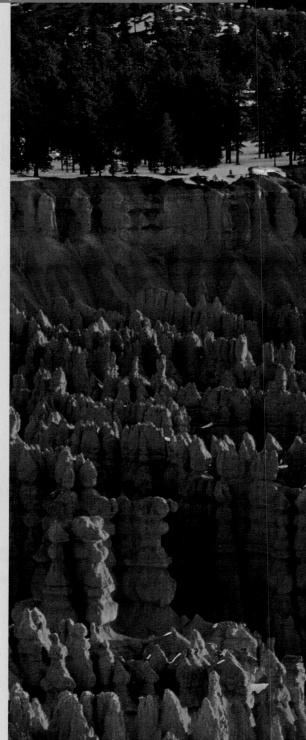

Where Is Our Country?

Mrs. Banks makes maps.
The maps show **continents** and **oceans**.
A continent is a large piece of land.
An ocean is a big body of water.
Our country is part of North America.

Find the United States of America on the map.
Mexico is south of the United States.
Which country is north of the United States?

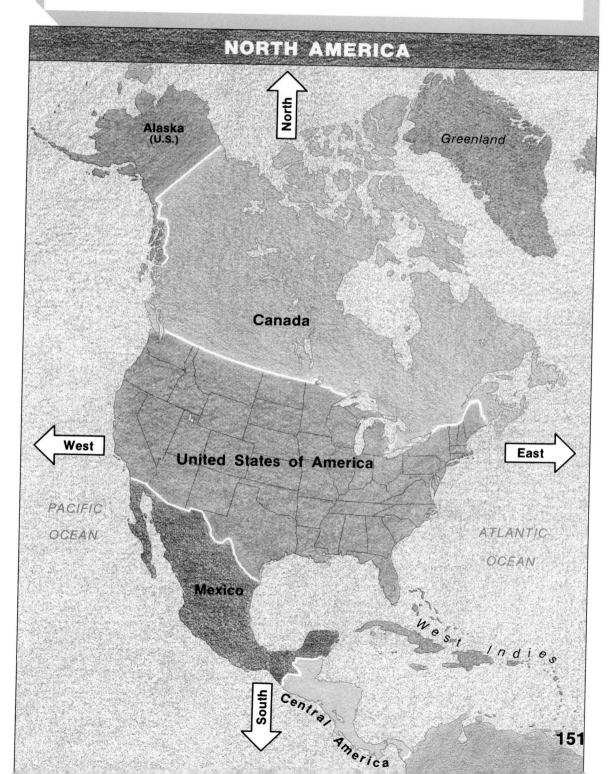

NORTH AMERICA

North

Alaska
(U.S.)

Greenland

Canada

West

East

United States of America

PACIFIC
OCEAN

ATLANTIC
OCEAN

Mexico

West Indies

South Central America

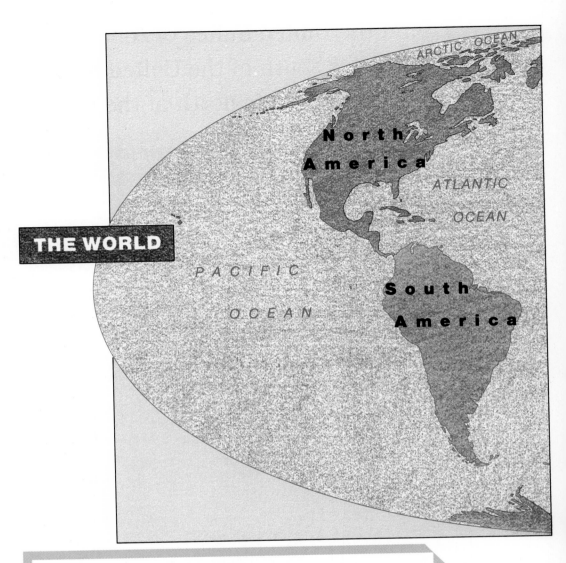

THE WORLD

Here is a world map.
Find the four oceans on the map.
Each continent is a different color
on this map.
How many continents are there?

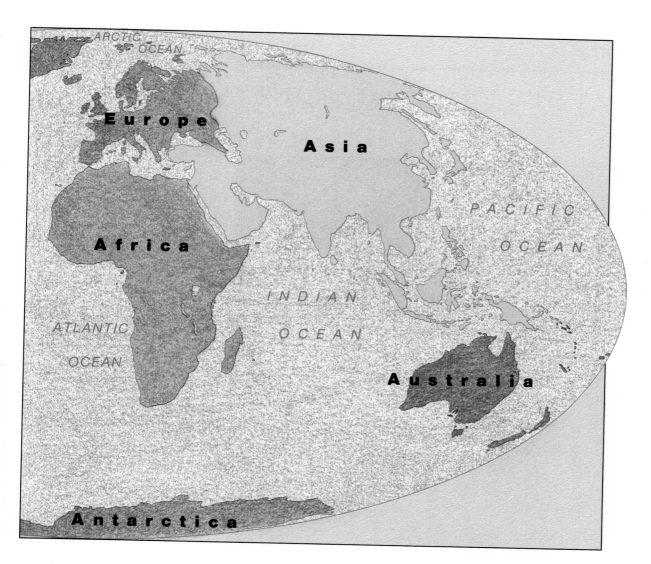

Lesson 1

Review

Read and Think

1. What is a continent?
2. How many oceans are there?

Skills Check

Look at the map on page 151.

What ocean is west of the United States?

Who Are Our Country's Leaders?

Our country has many leaders.
Sometimes many people want to be leaders.
The people in our country vote.
Voting is a way to choose leaders.
The people who get the most votes
become the leaders.

Our President is an important leader.
We vote for our President every four years.
The President lives and works in the White House.
The White House is in Washington, D.C.
Washington, D.C., is the capital of our country.
Many leaders work in Washington, D.C.

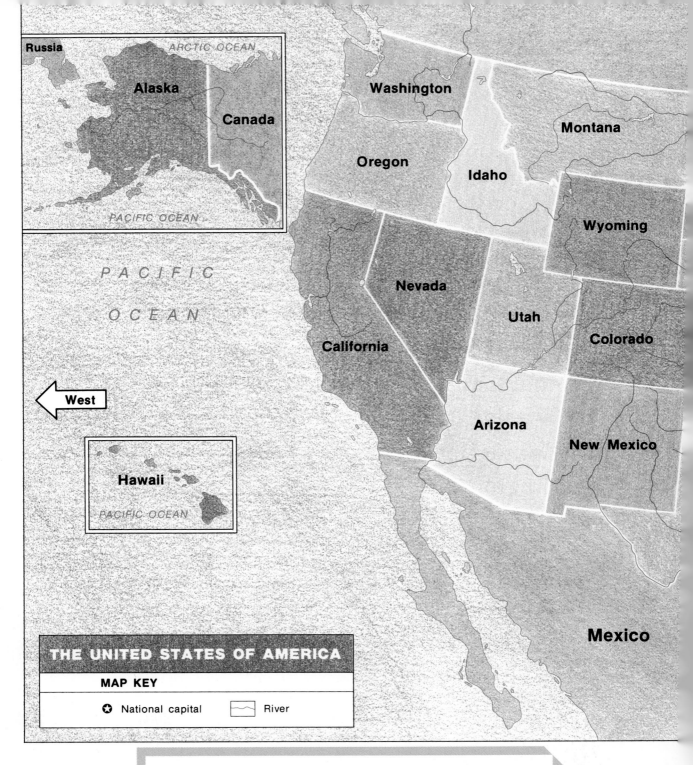

Russia

ARCTIC OCEAN

Alaska

Canada

PACIFIC OCEAN

PACIFIC OCEAN

West

Hawaii

PACIFIC OCEAN

Washington

Oregon

Idaho

Montana

Nevada

Utah

Wyoming

Colorado

California

Arizona

New Mexico

Mexico

THE UNITED STATES OF AMERICA

MAP KEY

✪ National capital   River

This is a map of the United States.
Can you find Washington, D.C.?

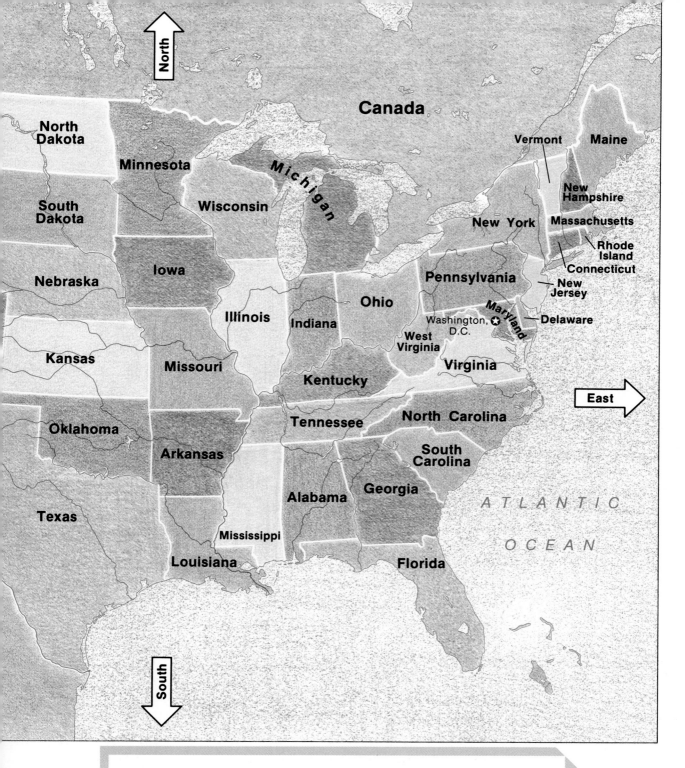

The United States has fifty main parts.

Each part is called a **state**.

Each state sends leaders to the capital.

One group of leaders in Washington, D.C., is called **Congress**.

Congress makes **laws** for the whole country.

A law is a rule for our country.

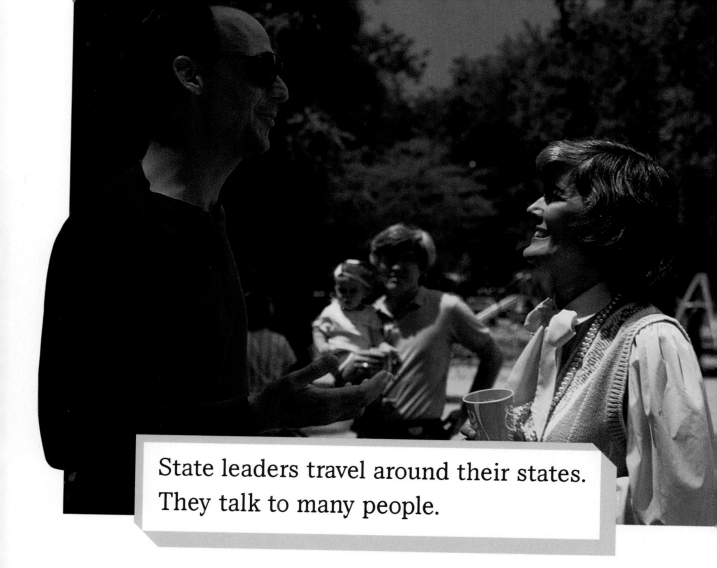

State leaders travel around their states. They talk to many people.

Lesson 2 — Review

Read and Think

1. Who makes laws for our country?
2. Why should people vote for their leaders?

Skills Check

Look at the map on pages 156 and 157.
What state is north of Oregon?

What Makes Each State Special?

Washington, D.C., is our country's capital city.
Each state has a capital city too.
The leaders for each state meet in the capital city.
They make laws for the state.
This picture shows the building where the
leaders in Indiana meet.

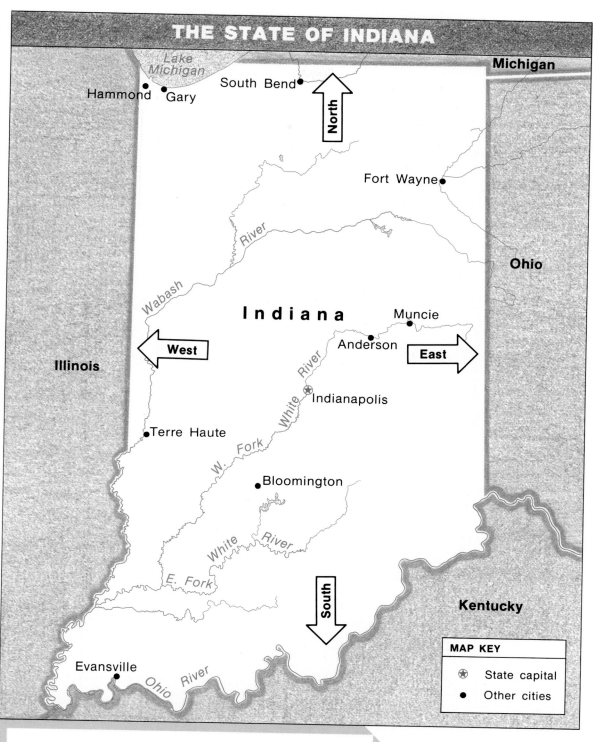

THE STATE OF INDIANA

Michigan

Lake Michigan

Hammond • Gary • South Bend •

North

Fort Wayne •

Ohio

Wabash River

Indiana

Muncie •

Anderson •

West

East

Illinois

White River

⊛ Indianapolis

• Terre Haute

W. Fork

• Bloomington

White River

E. Fork

South

Kentucky

Evansville • Ohio River

MAP KEY

⊛ State capital

• Other cities

What is the capital of Indiana?

Each state has a special tree and flower.
There is a flag for each state too.
These things are special to Indiana.
Do you know what things are special
to your state?

Some states have sports teams.
Many people watch basketball in Indiana.
Does your state have a sports team?

Lesson 3 ——————— Review ———————

Read and Think

1. Where are the laws for each state made?
2. How are the states alike?

Skills Check

Look at the map on page 161.
What city is south of Terre Haute?

Lesson 4

What Are Our Country's Symbols?

A **symbol** reminds us of something else.
There are symbols for our country.
The eagle is a symbol of our country.

The flag is a symbol
of our country too.
Symbols say that our
country is special to us.

The Star-Spangled Banner

Music by John Stafford Smith
Words by Francis Scott Key

Oh, — say! can you see, by the dawn's ear - ly light,

What so proud - ly we hailed at the twi - light's last gleam - ing,

Whose broad stripes and bright stars, through the per - il - ous fight,

O'er the ram - parts we watched were so gal - lant - ly stream - ing?

And the rock - ets' red glare, the bombs burst - ing in air,

Gave proof through the night that our flag was still there.

Oh, say, does that — Star - Span - gled Ban - ner — yet — wave —

O'er the land — of the free and the home of the brave?

Words and songs can be symbols too.
We sing "The Star-Spangled Banner."
It is our national anthem.
We say the Pledge of Allegiance.

Pledge of Allegiance to the Flag of the United States

I pledge allegiance to the flag
of the United States of America
and to the Republic for which it stands,
one Nation under God, indivisible,
with liberty and justice for all.

Some symbols of our country mean freedom.
The Liberty Bell is a symbol of freedom.
People came to this country to be free.
The bell was rung to tell people that
they would be free.
You can see the bell in Philadelphia.

The Statue of Liberty is another symbol.
The statue welcomes people to our country.
It reminds us of freedom.

Review

Read and Think

1. What is a symbol?
2. Where do you see symbols of our country?

Skills Check

Look at the pictures on pages 164 and 165.
Name the symbols of our country.

What Are Natural Resources?

Our country has **natural resources**.
Air, water, and land are natural resources.
Farmers need air, water, and land to grow crops.

Mike's mother works in a forest.
She takes care of the trees.
Trees are another natural resource.

Trees are used to make many things.
Mike has a pen pal named Jomo.
Jomo's family works with resources too.

Dear Mike,

My family grows corn on a small farm.
Many people grow corn in Kenya.
People eat corn with many meals.
My family eats most of the corn we grow.
We sell some of the corn.
Our land is important to my family.

Your friend,
Jomo

People need clean air and water to live.
Workers help to keep these resources clean.
Each of us can help too.

Lesson 5 ——————— Review ——————

Read and Think

1. Name some natural resources.
2. What can you do to keep our air and water clean?

Skills Check

Farmers use our natural resources.
Write a story about being a farmer.

How Can We Save Our Resources?

Trees are a natural resource.

We must use our trees carefully.

We need to let some trees grow.

They help our land and our air.

We need to use other trees to make things.

174

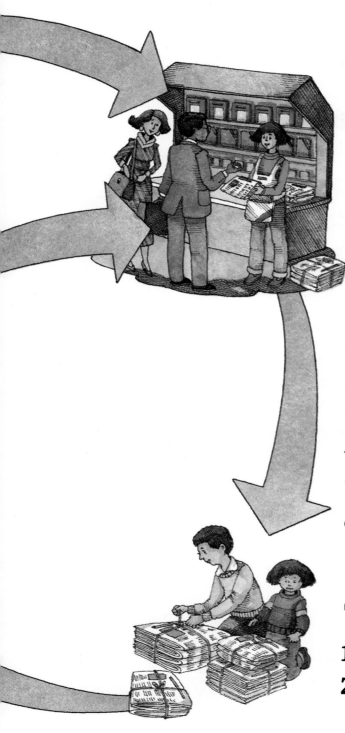

Find the trees in the picture.
Some of the trees go
to a paper factory.
Newspapers are printed on some
of the paper.
People buy newspapers to read.
Newspapers can be used again,
so people save them.
The newspapers go to
another factory.
This factory takes the ink
off of the paper.
Then the paper can be used
to make new newspapers.
This helps to save one of
our natural resources.

Thinking for Yourself

1. Why do we need trees?
2. How can your family help
   to save resources?

A. Using the New Words

Find the picture that best matches each word.

1. law _____
2. ocean _____
3. state _____
4. symbol _____
5. natural resources _____
6. Congress _____
7. continents _____

A.

B.

C.

D.

E.

F.

G.

176

B. Remembering What You Read

Answer these questions about the unit.

1. The United States is on which continent?
2. How does our country pick leaders?
3. Look at the pictures on this page.
   How are the symbols different?

C. Summarizing the Unit

Draw a picture of a place you have visited in our country.
Why is this place special to you?
In which state is your special place?

Identifying Landforms

 A ## Why Do I Need This Skill?

The earth has water and land.
Water and land make landforms.
This lesson will help you name
landforms that you see.

B ## Learning the Skill

The picture shows four kinds of landforms.
An island is land with water all around it.
A lake is a body of water with land around it.
A hill is higher than the land around it.
A mountain is a very high hill.

C Practicing the Skill

Look at the pictures on this page.

1. Which picture shows a lake?
2. Which picture shows a hill?
3. Which picture shows an island?
4. Which picture shows a mountain?

d.

a.

b.

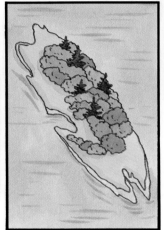

c.

D Applying the Skill

You are going on a trip to an island.
Name some ways to get to the island.
Why might going to an island be
harder than going to a lake?

Unit 7

OUR COUNTRY'S HOLIDAYS

New Words

holiday

celebrate

feast

Pilgrims

American Indians

Why Do We Celebrate Columbus Day?

Columbus Day is a **holiday**.
Holidays help us remember special times.
They help us remember special people too.
We remember Christopher Columbus
on Columbus Day.

Christopher Columbus lived long ago.
He lived in a country called Spain.
Columbus was a sea captain.
He led three ships across the
Atlantic Ocean.
Columbus was one of the first people
to make this trip.

The Granger Collection

Columbus found new land near our country. Other people came to the new land after Christopher Columbus.

The Granger Collection

We **celebrate** Columbus Day on October 12.
We remember his famous trip.

Review

Read and Think

1. Who was Christopher Columbus?
2. Why would sailors go with Columbus?

Skills Check

Look at the picture on page 184.
What did the ships need to move?

FROM

COLUMBUS

BY INGRI AND EDGAR PARIN D'AULAIRE

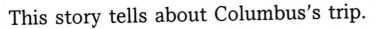

This story tells about Columbus's trip.

The sailors are looking for land.

How do the sailors know that land is near?

Days went by; weeks went by. They sailed on and on
and saw nothing but the desolate sea and sky.

At last, one day, they spied a strange object in the water.

It was a carved stick.

Soon afterward a sailor fished up a branch
with buds and flowers.

The salty air seemed sweet and fragrant in their nostrils,
as if scented already by the spices of India.

Next day great flocks of land birds flew over the masts.

Land must be near.

For the first time Columbus changed his command.

He called, "To the southwest," and followed the birds.

Now every man was peering ahead.

Late at night, while Columbus stood at his lonely watch, staring through the dark, it seemed to him that one of the stars, low in the sky, looked different from the others.

It didn't twinkle.

It flickered like the flame of a candle.

It could not be a star.

It must be a fire kindled by man.

Columbus called his men.

They all saw it.

He ordered the anchors dropped so the ships would not hit a reef in the night.

Before dawn a cannon shot boomed.

It was a signal from the *Pinta,* which was ahead.

Her crew had seen breakers and a dark coast line.

It was Friday, October 12, 1492.

What Do You Think?

How, do you think, did Columbus feel when they found land?

Why Is Thanksgiving Celebrated?

The **Pilgrims** came to our country long ago.
They left their homes in Europe.
They wanted to live in a new land.

The Pilgrims built homes and planted crops.
American Indians were living in our country.
They helped the Pilgrims with their crops.

There was a **feast** when the crops were grown.
The Pilgrims and the Indians ate together.
The Pilgrims thanked God for their food.
They thanked God for their friends too.
This was the first Thanksgiving.

Today Thanksgiving is a holiday in November. People remember what they are thankful for.

Review

Read and Think

1. Why did the Pilgrims have a feast?
2. What are you thankful for?

Skills Check

Think about the Pilgrims and the Indians.
Write a story about the first Thanksgiving.

Who Are Some People We Honor?

Long ago laws for our country were made
in England.
Our country wanted to make its own laws.
The countries could not agree, so there
was a war.
George Washington helped our country win.
He became our first President.

Abraham Lincoln was another President.
Our country had a problem.
Some states did not want to be part
of our country.
President Lincoln kept our country together.

Our country is proud of Lincoln and
Washington.
We remember them on Presidents' Day.
There are special places to honor them
in Washington, D.C.

Martin Luther King, Jr., was another leader.
He wanted everyone to be treated fairly.
There is a holiday to remember his dream.

<u>Lesson 3</u> ——————— **Review** ———————

Read and Think

1. Whom do we remember on Presidents' Day?
2. How do we show we are proud of people?

Skills Check

Look at the pictures on pages 194 and 196.
What symbol of our country do you see on both pages?

What Is Flag Day?

We celebrate Flag Day on June 14.
We honor the American flag.
Many homes fly our flag on the holiday.

The first flag was made by hand.
Some people think that Betsy Ross made
the first flag.
The flag was planned by our first Congress.
The colors red, white, and blue were picked.
Congress wanted stars and stripes on the flag.

Long ago our country only had 13 states.
The first flag had 13 stars and 13 stripes.
Today our flag still has 13 stripes.
They remind us of the first 13 states.
Now there are 50 stars on our flag.
There is a star for each state.

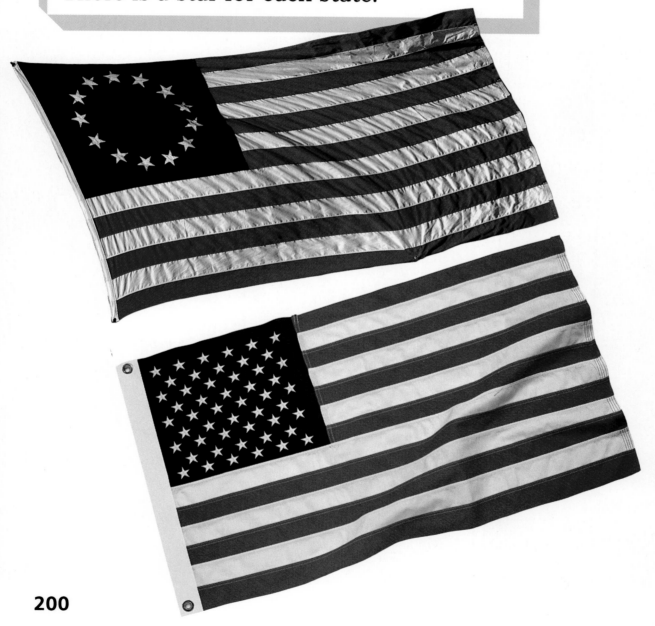

Our flag is a symbol
of our country.
We are proud of our
country on Flag Day.

Lesson 4

Review

Read and Think

1. What did the first flag look like?
2. What kind of flag would you make for our country?

Skills Check

Look at the pictures on page 200.
How are the flags alike?

A. Using the New Words

Find the picture that best matches each word.

1. American Indians ____

2. celebrate ____

3. Pilgrims ____

4. holiday ____

5. feast ____

A.

B.

C.

D.

E.

B. **Remembering What You Read**

Answer these questions about the unit.

1. Why do people celebrate holidays?
2. Name some ways people celebrate holidays.
3. How are the people we honor alike?
   How are they different?

 C. **Summarizing the Unit**

Write a story about your favorite holiday.
How do you celebrate the holiday?
Draw a picture of your celebration.

SKILLBUILDER

Using a Time Line

 A **Why Do I Need This Skill?**

Time lines show when events happened.
Some things happened long ago.
Some things just happened.
Time lines help us see the order of events.

 B **Learning the Skill**

Look at the time line on this page.
It shows important events in Mary's family.
The time line starts when Mary was born.
Each box is one year on this time line.
Mary was one when her family got a dog.

Born | 1 year old | 2 years old | 3 years old | 4 years old | 5 years old | 6 years old

New dog   New house   New baby School

204

C Practicing the Skill

This time line shows holidays during the
school year.
Each box is one month on this time line.
The first holiday is Columbus Day.
What holiday comes in June?

September October November December January

Columbus Thanksgiving   Martin Luther
Day   King, Jr., Day

February March April May June

Presidents'   Flag Day
Day

D Applying the Skill

Make a time line of your life.
Make each box stand for one year.
Put at least one event in each box.

ATLAS

Russia

ARCTIC OCEAN

Alaska

Canada

Anchorage

Juneau

PACIFIC

OCEAN

West

Pearl City • Honolulu

Hawaii

PACIFIC
OCEAN

C a n a d a

• Seattle

Olympia

Portland • **Washington**

Salem

Oregon

Helena **Montana**

• Billings

Boise

Idaho

Pocatello •

Wyoming

Casper •

Cheyenne

Carson City

Sacramento

West
Valley • Salt Lake
City

Nevada

Utah

River

Denver •

Colorado

Colorado
Springs

California

Las Vegas •

Colorado

Los Angeles •

Arizona

Santa Fe •

Albuquerque •

Phoenix •

New Mexico

Tucson •

M e x i c o

THE UNITED STATES OF AMERICA

MAP KEY

✪ National capital

✪ State capitals

• Other cities

North Dakota
Fargo
Bismarck

Minnesota

South Dakota
Pierre
Sioux Falls

St. Paul
Minneapolis

Wisconsin
Milwaukee
Madison

Canada

Lake Superior

Michigan

Lake Huron

Lansing
Detroit

Lake Michigan

Nebraska
Omaha
Lincoln

Iowa
Cedar Rapids
Des Moines

Chicago

Illinois
Springfield

Fort Wayne

Indiana
Indianapolis

Cleveland

Ohio
Columbus

Lake Erie

Maine
Augusta
Montpelier
Burlington
Portland
New Hampshire
Vermont Concord
Albany Nashua **Massachusetts**
Boston Worcester
New York Hartford Plymouth
Bridgeport Providence
Warwick
Newark **Rhode Island**
New York **Connecticut**
Trenton
Pennsylvania **New Jersey**
Harrisburg Philadelphia
Baltimore Wilmington
Annapolis Dover
Washington, D.C. **Delaware**
Maryland

Kansas
Topeka
Wichita

Missouri
Kansas City
Jefferson City

Louisville

Frankfort

Kentucky

Huntington

West Virginia
Charleston

Richmond

Virginia
Virginia Beach

East

Oklahoma
Tulsa
Oklahoma City

Fort Smith

Arkansas
Little Rock

Memphis

Nashville

Tennessee

Raleigh

North Carolina
Charlotte

Missouri River

Mississippi River

Texas
Austin
Houston

Mississippi
Jackson

Baton Rouge
New Orleans

Louisiana

Biloxi

Birmingham

Alabama
Montgomery

Atlanta

Georgia
Columbus

South Carolina
Columbia

Charleston

ATLANTIC

Jacksonville
Tallahassee
St. Augustine

OCEAN

Florida

Gulf of Mexico

North

South

ATLAS

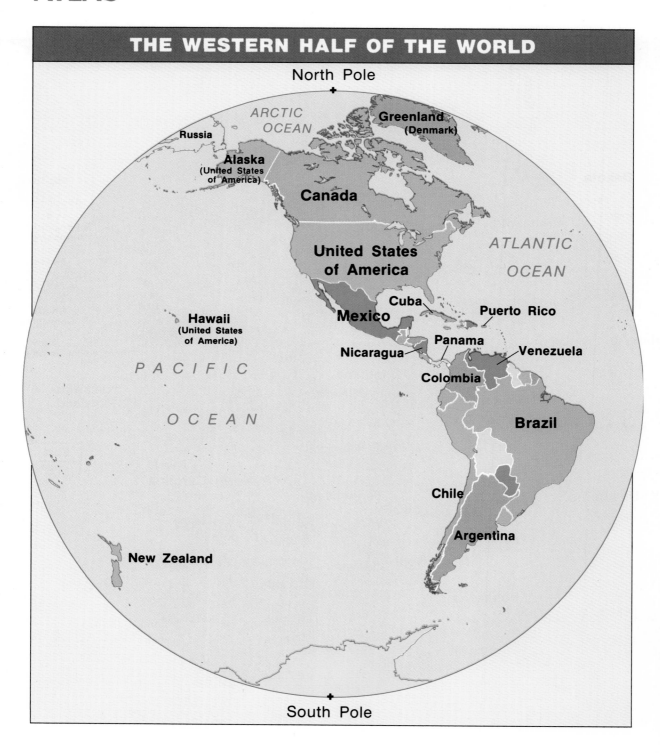

THE WESTERN HALF OF THE WORLD

North Pole

✛

ARCTIC
OCEAN

Greenland
(Denmark)

Russia

Alaska
(United States
of America)

Canada

United States
of America

ATLANTIC

OCEAN

Cuba

Puerto Rico

Hawaii
(United States
of America)

Mexico

Panama

Venezuela

Nicaragua

Colombia

PACIFIC

Brazil

OCEAN

Chile

Argentina

New Zealand

✛

South Pole

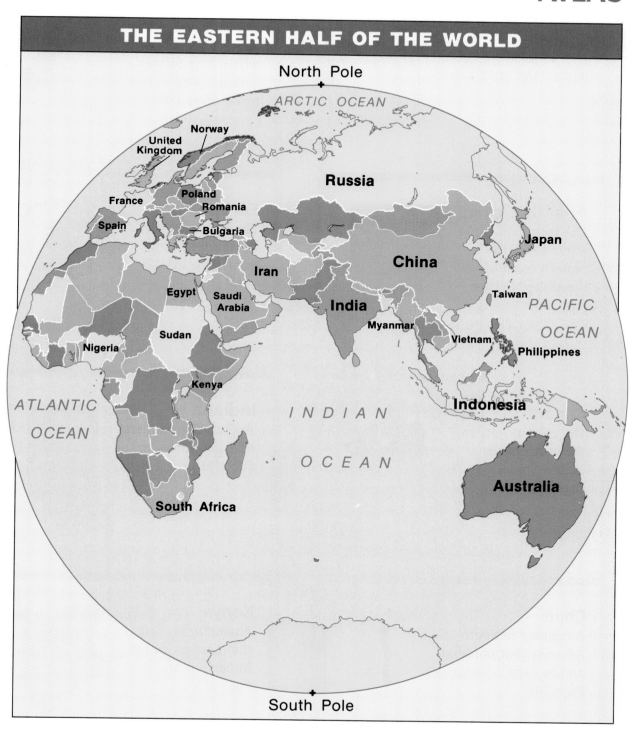

THE EASTERN HALF OF THE WORLD

North Pole

ARCTIC OCEAN

Norway

United Kingdom

Russia

France

Poland

Romania

Japan

Spain

Bulgaria

Iran

China

Egypt

Saudi Arabia

India

Taiwan

PACIFIC OCEAN

Sudan

Myanmar

Nigeria

Vietnam

Philippines

Kenya

Indonesia

ATLANTIC OCEAN

INDIAN OCEAN

Australia

South Africa

South Pole

DICTIONARY OF PLACES

You can find each of these places on a map in your book. The page numbers tell you where the maps are.

England
The part of the United Kingdom where laws for our country used to be made. Page 209

Atlantic Ocean
The large body of water along the eastern coast of the United States. Page 151

Europe
The continent that the Pilgrims came from. Page 153

Canada
The country just to the north of the United States. Page 151

Indiana
A state that borders on Lake Michigan. Page 161

Chile
A country in South America that borders on the Pacific Ocean. Page 208

Kenya
A country in Africa that borders on the Indian Ocean. Page 209

London
The capital city of the United Kingdom. Page 209

Spain
The country that Christopher Columbus sailed from. Page 209

Mexico
The country just to the south of the United States. Page 151

United States of America
Our country, which stretches from the Atlantic Ocean to the Pacific Ocean. Pages 156–157

North America
The continent that our country is part of. Page 151

Washington, D.C.
Our country's capital city. Page 157

Philadelphia
A large city in Pennsylvania where the Liberty Bell is found. Page 207

West Virginia
A state in the eastern part of the United States. Page 157

PICTURE GLOSSARY

alike

Twins look **alike**.   Page 18

alone

Sometimes Jim works **alone**.   Page 26

American Indians

American Indians knew how to grow crops.   Page 191

apartment

My new **apartment** is in a tall building.   Page 67

B   bar graph

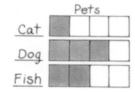

This **bar graph** tells about pets.   Page 80

C   celebrate

We **celebrate** my birthday each year.   Page 185

change

Moving was a **change** for my family.   Page 38

city

A **city** is a busy place.
Page 139

clothing

Pants are one kind of **clothing**. Page 61

community

My **community** has many stores. Page 126

Congress

Congress makes laws for all of us. Page 158

continent

Our country is part of a **continent**. Page 150

D

different

Sue and Mike look **different**. Page 19

directions

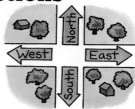

There are four main **directions**. Page 120

F

factory

This **factory** makes books. Page 96

family

My **family** is a special group of people. Page 34

farm

We have animals on our **farm**. Page 50

PICTURE GLOSSARY

feast

We had a **feast** on Thanksgiving.   Page 192

food

There are many kinds of **food** to eat.   Page 60

G **globe**

You can find our country on a **globe**.   Page 24

goods

Many **goods** are made in factories.   Page 92

group

This **group** will play together.   Page 26

H **holiday**

The Fourth of July is a **holiday**.   Page 182

L **law**

The **law** says to stop at a red light.   Page 158

M **map**

I need a **map** to find Jim's house.   Page 44

map key

The **map key** will help me find the house. Page 44

 natural resources

Trees and water are **natural resources**. Page 170

needs

Food is one of our **needs**. Page 60

neighbor

I wave to my **neighbor** every day. Page 118

neighborhood

My friends live in my **neighborhood**. Page 118

 ocean

I like to watch the waves in the **ocean**. Page 150

P **pictograph**

The **pictograph** tells about going to school. Page 98

Pilgrims

The **Pilgrims** sailed to our country. Page 190

 rule

My class made a **rule** about the crayons. Page 12

PICTURE GLOSSARY

school

I learn many things in **school**. Page 4

service

The dentist gives a **service**. Page 94

shelter

We are looking for a new **shelter**. Page 61

state

West Virginia is a **state**. Page 157

symbol

The eagle is a **symbol** of our country. Page 164

table

Kinds of Clothing		
Clothing	Summer	Winter
Shorts	X	
Mittens		X

This **table** shows different kinds of clothing. Page 142

travel

I like to **travel** on airplanes. Page 108

wants

Bikes and skates are **wants** for some children. Page 62

CREDITS